AN IMMORTAL NIGHTINGALE

20 POEMS IN ENGLISH

SREEVIDHYA S

Made with ♥ on the Notion Press Platform
www.notionpress.com

To the divinity around me for all my gifts!

To legends of English poetry for inspiring me to write in English!

To Appa K.B.Subramanian of Koduvayur, Kerala (Retd.Tamil pandit,poet and Veena Vidwan) my first inspiration through his fine handwriting, knowledge,music and love to me.

To Amma H.Mahalakshmi of Thiruvaiyaru, Tamilnadu

(Vibrant Homemaker)

She made me strong. I inherit her voice.

To Thangavel Sir, my affectionate teacher in 3rd class (P.U.Primary School, Gudalur, Nilgiris) for his good teaching that I started loving English

To Nataraj Sir, my English Teacher in 6th and 7th classes (Govt.Higher Secondary School, Gudalur, Nilgiris) who strengthened my English with his effective teaching

To Dr.Anusmitha Mam for her fine foreword

And

S.Anvershaji and S.A.Thamizh Ezhil for being my best critics, my family and my strength!

Contents

Foreword

Dr.Anusmitha Sebastian is an avid patron of Literature Studies and an academician passionate about Literary enterprise, Language dynamics and mechanisms to address social injustices. As a writer of poetry and short stories herself, she has put in 25 years of teaching and serves currently as Associate Professor and Head, Department of English, Government Arts and Science College for Women, Puliyakulam, Coimbatore, Tamilnadu.She is always enthusiastic to encourage good art and meaningful expression for the betterment of appalling conditions of humanity and Nature.‘’’‘’’

One of the most pertinent factors that our divided and broken world is in need of is balanced, composed and steady activist thinkers with long-standing vision and commitment towards fellow men's realities.

Ms. S. Sreevidhya is one such exemplary visionary with a penchant for language and highly sensitive insight into lives and living. It has been my honour to be associated with Ms.S.Sreevidhya through a friendship that was forged after a chance meeting years ago at an academic forum. Since then, I have developed respect and regards for the intellectual in her.

This anthology of poems aptly titled An Immortal Nightingale urge me to put the accent on the singularity of 'an' to wish Ms.Sreevidhya an immortality in her poetry and translation journey as a songster of the needs the hour many.Beginning with a statement on how a Poem is not to be apologised about but celebrated, she embarks on an intense social pilgrimage with persevering goodwill for the deprived and unjustly treated in the shadows.

A"SHE" Exothermic underlines the singular will of the lady at the hearth with a heart that undertakes to beat for humanity. A tribute to vulnerable and butchered cows reminds us ironically of the yoke of social burden imposed through Burden.

Choice is a sisterhood empathy with the know-how of the drudgery of Afghan women from a voice that aware and breathes freer, rebellion possible air.

The necessary wear and tear of the Self using a footwear metaphor drives home the impossibility of expelling the dull self as the writer muses on In and Out.

Train Beggars could not have captured more sarcastically the train ambience of ogling, judging, snobbish, condescending and livelihood seeking India. When the world loses an iconic social activist and young achiever like Pop Queen Nazia Hassan of the Aap Jaisa Koi Mere and Disco Deewaane fame, to mystery and cancer a tribute is due, beyond language boundaries and ethnicity, to the deserving voice more so in Tamil translation to English.

A teaching mother's guilty predicament, the nostalgia of a Blue Mountain childhood, the irony of chastising for chastity, the hope for a violence devoid gadget – engrossed world, the enormity of atrocity against children, the black wheel barricade in a lively friendship, it's suppressed vivacity the regretted meaninglessness in an infatuation driven monotonous marriage, and loss of good things or facts and features that find expression in this collection of poems.

The flip side of a useful tree being cut down is the sweeping obligation that an invalid is released from. Such nuances and attention to detail are noteworthy.

A typical lazy Sunday in the hustle and bustle of the late Nineties is celebrated while due consciousness given to the bondage of a pet in the scene.

The craft that the writer has for drawing the raw and basic beauty of the Indian milieu is evident from the description that no matter how imbalanced the sexes are, love alone rules, that no matter how many boy experiences were enjoyed on a roadside bridge, the girl who got no such freedom grew up to register a poem about it for eternity, and that Corona the mass equaliser emerged to teach mankind many a bitter lesson.

The reference to Nature, flowers, trees, plants, practices and experiences specific to the region give the poems a flavor of authenticity that is not lost in translation.

Writing is an intimate process for this multi-linguist who sheds her fire with ease on to paper.

The poems reach the reader the freshness of insight and perspective. The adeptness with which Ms. S.Sreevidhya waltzes from Tamil and English is praiseworthy and knowing her to be a recognized and awarded writer of Tamil works of significance, I congratulate her on her maiden venture into translating her poems meticulously and passionately. Pain, irony, pathos, agony, mind-blowing realities going unnoticed and bold celebrations of human grit to overcome and survive the blatant harm done by generations and systems find strong registering in her works. I wish the writer and fiery thinker in her many more ventures and successes. May all she undertakes meet its mark in the reading thinking world that relates with her.

Dr.Anusmitha Sebastian is an avid patron of Literature Studies and an academician passionate about Literary enterprise, Language dynamics and mechanisms to address social injustices. As a writer of poetry and short stories herself, she has put in 25 years of teaching and serves currently as Associate Professor and Head, Department of English, Government Arts and Science College for Women, Puliyakulam, Coimbatore, Tamilnadu.

She is always enthusiastic to encourage good art and meaningful expression for the betterment of appalling conditions of humanity and Nature.

Preface

S Sreevidhya

About the author

S.Sreevidhya, Assistant professor of English is a poet, short story writer, orator and translator. She is a voracious reader since young.

Four of her translation works have been published.

Awards: 'Woman of Excellence 2010' by 'Hello FM, Coimbatore.

'Best Cultural Co-Ordinator' by 'Deiva Tamil Sangam' Chennai.

'Best Faculty 2014' by Selvam College of Technology, Namakkal.

'Abdul Kalam', 'Bharathi' 'Vaagaikkavi' and 'Pongu Thamizh Kavi' awards from private Literary Associations.

Published works: 14 poems and 7 short stories (prize winners) in Tamil.

Won prize for a 'Novella' in an International Competition conducted by 'Kaakkai Cirakinilae' magazine in Tamil, yet to be published.

The poems in this collection are originally written in Tamil and translated into English by the author herself.

Continues writing poems and short stories in Tamil besides translation works in English, Malayalam and Sanskrit, feasible in future.

1. POEM

An excellent poem is
An eternal light of great joy!
Do not ever lament!
Gangrenous wounds
Would stain the new sheets
And whichever stained
Will be sought after by insects around.
Make yourself afresh!

2. A 'SHE' Exothermic

Summer in the city burns me
And my fellow man
Hungry every time, poverty burns me
And my fellow man
People die somewhere in burning fire
Affect me and my fellow man
The economy of my nation annoys me
And my fellow man
Every exothermic is for everyone
Except the stove meant for me alone
Burns me alone and extorts the soul –
It injects the sheepish regression
Into the opposing brains, mine too
I do boil over injustices,
Lest I should come out
From the heat of stove
The next meal to be cooked
Awaits me always
I will only keep on cooking
Till my fellow man
Volunteers himself to it
I will be the lost ship
Of the Bermuda – triangle,

And an unidentified island
Upon the globe's surface
All alone till release,
Yet to be identified
Till Time restores 'me' in 'me',
May be till the end of Cosmos!

3. BURDEN

Cows struggle to scamper
With fettered feet and
Dogs do run
Still stoned and limp –
So many dogs so far.
Crossing leagues –
Lassitude in paralysis,
To be butchered,
Cows are culpable –
They are cunningless.
Be it hay stack,
Banana bunches,
Or a human family –
Not that back breaking!
Is it so onerous
As the human dominance
Imposed for centuries?

4. CHOICE

(A poem dedicated to the women of Afghanistan)

Who wants all your virtues?
Would you endure anything?
No idea of avow?
Are you quidding sheep
To be nuzzled –
Everyone to relish upon
Your existence?
You may not be aware of
A disastrous foot fall;
For you have lost
Your 'self' earlier –
It's just a null body
To be blotted out!
Are you lionesses
To fight off till the end?
You end up in your war-field,
And it is plausible too,
You may triumph over the enemy!

5. In-Out

On day one
Mind willed not
. To wear the new footwear;
And it was not liked
Aftermath it bit the toe.
It become my feet
When got accustomed to-
'Why dirt it unnecessarily'
Wanted to unfasten
Whenever I sat down.
Got thrust with mud and rain,
It turned dull;
It was then I give a damn
It soon worn out,
The day to throw it out
Is not far away.
I too, often stuck in crooked thoughts
Worn out to swerve
To turn horrendous
My exterior shows no interior-
'I' am in 'Me' and
I can't throw 'Me' away-
Who gets rid of 'Self'?

6. Bonsais

When the verdant trees of protected area
go on spreading their branches
To propose love exudingly to the wind -
Why not the bonsais speak up?
That budding sproutings are shown mudpots
As straw calf is used to milk a cow
And violently shrunk into bonsais!
Bonsais of Nigeria
The genitals of whom are
Mutilated by rusty razors
Subdued since ages,
Cruise and crawl within with hard hearts –
Why not the bonsais speak up?
Why not they tell everyone?

7. Train Beggars

She is seen sitting by the steps
Of Palakkad passenger-
Her blouse half open
With safety pins imprisoned
To a duplicate chain and
Had a baby that was stunning
Nothing to find in between
Her linen saree someone gave,
And face unknown
As to whom it belongs,
She possessed a care free attitude
Unlike the churidar woman,
Glancing through the window
With a cheer forced.
The train moved and
She came singing in Hindi
'Pardesi Pardesi Jaana nahin'
Addressing him who left her alone-
(Oh, Stranger, don't go away
Leaving me behind-)
Hands held out for alms.
Hardly three years since bloomed,
Her breasts with no milk

To which the baby banged against.
Middle aged women stared and stared
As if they are watching a T.V series,
And gossiped that
The baby is not hers.
The man who laid straight
Ignoring those who were standing
The mother who eye-signaled
Her young lads window seated
To sit wide
The man who I caught
Staring below my neck
Turned to his wife's side
And inquired if she was hungry
The perfumed man shrunk back
When the dark-skinned sat by-
The railway cop did not sing any-
Stretched out his hand
Towards the flower seller lady
To snatch a twenty rupee, note.
The man who bent down
To a magazine's mid page picture of an actress,
People who turned to the news
In a serious manner- except these, although late
Most of them offered coins.
I wrote a poem and
My house is humming

The woe of her song.

8. Naziya, An Immortal Nightingale

'If a man like you
Walks into my life,
It's not a sin
To abandon the songs
Born of my soul -
A tender Nightingale refusing songs,
That was me!
Trusted your words,
That you would hand me your heart,
I strangled my music,
Killed it in silence.
'I love you alone, not your fame'
You kept on telling me.
I do not grasp the untold sense.
My Indian fame
Would have set ablaze
The wild fire of Indonesia
In you!
'Id-Mubarak's and 'Iftar's aside,
My vocal cords hurt
With rest that was thrust -
My heart sobbed

Somewhere in a nook.
You could not have heard it,
No wonder!
My music had a flaw,
It had once wiped out the
Indo-Pak border lines-
Unable to reach you
Though you were nearby.
The soul was unsettled
With those lyrics
Like a half-severed 'halal' animal,
You freed it
By getting rid of me
In the ailing bed.
Death tells me that
Both began in the same day -
My lung cancer and
Your disease in the brain!
The journey of my sweet melodies
That are blocked in this world
Will resume in the Heaven!
And I will be re-born
In death alone!

In Memory of Naziya Hassan (cover photo)

Naziya Hassan (April 3, 1965 - August 13,2000) of 'Qurbani' fame (Aap jaisa koi meri zindagi mein aaye to baat ban jaye) left this world with a voice matchless.

She was known as the 'South Asian Queen of Pop' when she settled in Pakistan with her fundamentalist husband and quit singing.
Depressions from marital life and diagonised with lung cancer,
(Her husband had abandoned her by then!)
she died a lonely death in her ailing bed.

9. A Teacher's Journey

My kid's scribbling
Amid my notes of lessons
Are ecstatic –
Why do not I recall them?
In the broiling times
When I find fault with others!
The tender kid's eyes wet,
'Mom' he calls out
Lo, I get into the bus
Ignoring him solicit for a kiss
My days darken……
I set a journey
Disjoining a kid,
Towards hundreds of kids
To lighten the coming nights!

10. Road To College in The Nilgiris

Where the *lemurian flower-
The snake – like *kaanthal flourished,
The impartial mist is still overcast
The cash crops.
A remant mercy,
The now – crawling *Pandiyar –
A thirst – quencher once,
Might have been the melody
Of an eco – friendly past.
The journey curves enlighten us,
Wild stream flow amidst bushes
Echoing the bliss pushed off.
Tar road lies as an assaulted snake,
Has swollen crores:
Yet drive my abdomen to mouth.
Off my window often I watch
The silent procession of factory women -workers
(They always cook and come out
before the dawn sets in)
Pass behind well-nourished creepers of pepper,
With their faces of hunger.
Breeze brings me the flavor of tea

And it's nauseous to the mind.
There goes the veiled little girl
Out of the roadside Masjid
Holding a full-bloomed hi-biscus .
Hibiscus is cut down for fencing,
Flowers to pre-mature death and
Fresh ones to bathe by
Buses full of dust.
Proximity to tender hearts
Is not welcomed ;
Haunting walls every where
I know not to break
For they are invisible.
I do hope 'Let castles be built'
and wonder whether
the soul of high mountains
Rest above beyond reach,
Just intangible.

*Lemuria – A lost continent of the ethnic Tamils,believed to have sunk beneath the sea,
to the south of the Indian sub-continent,
also Known as 'Kumarikkandam'
*Kaanthal – A unique flower of 'Kurinji' land '
glorified in the 'Sangam' literature of Tamil.
The Nilgiris belong to 'Kurinji'.
*Pandiyar – A river flowing across the Nilgiris
of Tamilnadu and Kerala.

11. SIN

Chastity is imposed upon her
As ensilage in one eye
And extorted too –
They tell that
She allures in each attire
Why, her mere existence does!
The sinners themselves pelt stones!
Right now –
Jesus may descend from his cross!

12. Life in Gadgets

It is likely that
This could happen-
In search of material gain
Drown in mechanization,
In a life formatted
To win electronic gadgets
With waves of thoughts worn out,
This could happen,
The chain of gene meant for violence
Shall suddenly be sheared
And men may fail to recall
The color of blood and
Few people would still grumble-
News is not engrossing!

13. GROWTH

People who abandon a neo-natal
On the day of advent to the world,
For dogs of street to tear off,
People who would not cling to
Of paw kids who quiver
On their first bus journey,
People who turn cruelties into words
And downpour them with grins
Upon non- respondent school kids –
Assuming that they won't grasp,
And people who sexually assault
Some tender childhood
Are all 'grown-ups'!

14. Thahira, A Rabbit Kitty

She is a rabbit kitty of
An exuberant women's college
Where virtue is preferred
(As is always)
A humble princess
With a face of bloomed rose-
She gifts us
Morning , noon and evening wishes
All the while we come across
She hops, jumps and run through,
Verandahs and class rooms,
Rest rooms too not spared -
Spreading ever cheer.
She's excited at colours and
To sit upon the lap of
Her well-- built friend.
We discussed-
Trans-continental feminine awakening;
Yet her rabbit-kitty gestures
Had their grips over her.
Among university rank- holders
Those lights of neon shone on

Reflection of 'RAJOTHA' Dais
(Ramya , Jothi and Thahira)
Proclaimed who she is!
She proffered blessings
That touched her head ,
Her eyes tearful - smiled .
On the way in quest of knowledge
At the periods of heart-felt bond
Toward journeys ahead
Between She and Me
Barricades the giant ice-berg,
That full veil of black !
Neither male nor female ,
Just a soul –less black!
How on Earth would I
Tell her that I despise black !

15. A Stupor Subject

She is an amaranthine flower
Partly broken from the parental branch
She shows the same premature girl in face.
Until yesterday she had friends
And time-past sleep
Borne dreams in times of temperance,
Enters into the kitchen –
Cockroaches and the lizards of wall
Stained utensils and dirty doormats
Offer a welcome note.
Her man immersed into his mobile
Shows no facial signs -
Yester night's act of love.
Uncertain of the cooker's whistle,
Hot mustard spattered in the corner of eye'
Her table-serves with
Little finger hurt by the kitchen knife
After a half- bath
Without adoring herself
She dresses up with no choices
Skips her moments of
Smiling at the mirror image
Glancing him eat

She trowels and gulps
Her minor mouthfuls.
The honey drops of love
That dropped over WhatsApp
Just dissolves like syrup of sugar
By chores of harness
Continue with commas –
She is aware of it.
She rushes to her office
That is far,
Stumbling in sari,
Unfailingly catches the bus
Wondering the dictionary
That says
'Men and women belong
To the 'Human Race'!

16. Cause and Effect

They charge thus,
'A jamun tree is undesirable at house'
'Your building would crackle'
'Trash gathers; we can't sweep'
Those who received
Fruits with a smile mild
And those wanted the seed
For a diabetes husband
Read the indictment
'Cut down your tree first!'
The girl nicknamed 'jamun blackie'-
She loves to walk on fallen leaves
Seems annoyed and gets mad-
She shakes like a leaf.
Everybody's wind
Could not comprehend
With the human tongue.
The mother who
Devoured bowls of jamuns
When she had been to her natal house
Bearing the child
Is inert and just nods.
The father who glorified the bird voices

As old musical notes
Surrenders for he can't fracas.
The grandson's opinion not sought,
He used to be there set
Beneath the tree with a mug of water
To rinse to eat jamuns sweeter
In season ripe jamuns shed down.
There will be tiles
When he visits next.
The white flies and leaf worms
Insects' names not known
Crows and parrots
No lesser squirrels
Fed and lived on that tree.
When it fell to a sickle,
Where have they gone?
Do they exist or not,
Nobody knows.
I know of this,
The neighbor lady of backyard
Will not sweep her floor anymore,
She underwent a hysterectomy
And has become awry.

17. Cats and Dogs

Dogs wag tails even for mean people
And are out of favor
Cats are dear to me.
Pet cats are not submissive,
Personal space they crave -
Boundaries are not to be touched,
Trespassers get slapped in face.
Mind stops nowhere
Running like a tap that leaks
In hard quest for wealth
And wavering in and out-
Search of soul returns to the nest.
Always hurried to catch the bus-
After days six,
A day to wake up late
For a sweet second tea,
Mind-filling mid-day meal,
'Mahabharatham'or
A good movie,
Witty exchanges and
Moments of intimacy,
Move to a small rest.
But still in defiance to all these,

There rises an awful cry every day
Which I hear often in Sundays alone;
Acuity lowers into a whine
Like a new-born ignored,
It is ample to disrupt my quietude;
Begging those selective deaf humans
To unfasten that chain of slavery,
A life prisoner dog's howl!

18. LOVE

She is a soul abandoned
He is welcomed in turns
She ran after butterflies
He rode his vehicles
She shone with colours
He wore jeans rough
She stuck to household chores
He kicks to uphold his views
She is tender but labours hard
He is harder yet had leisures
She longs for her songs and romances
He leans for pride and lust
She and he fell in love
She cares and he cares
Such is the magic of love
Love alone whirls the world!

19. Reflections Upon a Bridge: 1984

A lass of fourteen passes the bridge.
At call distance 'It's raining twilight'
From her home radio, sings.
Men of different ages
Have occupied the bridge-wall;
Haste-free chats along.
Everyone assumes that
She is glancing at him and
Pucker lips to sound-out.
A goatherd 's heard
"Pretty lamb, isn't it?"
The same bridge was hers too,
Until grade six.
The ground grass and 'touch-me-not',
Phlomis for Lord Ganesh,
The creepers dark green
And flowers carrot-colored
Spread covering the roof of
Old electricity board building
Belonged her.
At the valley below the bridge
The day a snake's seen crisscrossing,

We drew our plaits close to scale
As to whose is longer-
That friend of mine needed no
Pills for mental fuss then.
We've oft seen Mumtaz
Giving up her veil
While she elapsed the bridge.
Ghost stories we exchanged-
After fun-watching the man of ridge house
Who hanged himself and swayed,
Might begotten form and be
Meandering there still.
The same twilight Sun,
The distant twin hills
Lie in her water color paintings
That are lost!
She had drunk that
Amber red bright.
The bridge was forbidden for her
When she is seen with school-mates (boys!)
And behavior spoken of.
'Lest a thorn could have pricked',
She would have passed by slowly-
The mind-nourishing evening arts!
'Women do not anyway
Bother to sit upon the bridge'
'Primitive Sun is common to all souls!'

This line is not meant for her?
Still, she grieves not,
For she alone-
Who was not fortunate enough
To sit upon the bridge round the seasons
Made it a theme,
A song for the bridge
Which morphed all her evenings
Into a drop of elixir!

Enter Caption

20. Regime of Corona

Times in vain have gone, gone.
Stimulations of bliss
From dawns setting in and
Oasis of dream flowers
Stopped aside –
Eaten with neither hunger nor taste,
Parted past polluted ranges
In search of fortune.
Falcons feeding upon the dead –
Dragging lies around,
Contagious hatred undress in haste
In hypnosis to taste flesh
And roam about the streets,
While some serve the souls there,
Those medic – models
Sans – seconds to care for their souls,
Array the cool great ray
As the earth's divine light!
Dusted in and out
Seek the lap of mother clean
Learn those not learnt
Though the time's out;
Elixir dribble by dribble

As precipitations in the desert.
Values added in silence
To every drop of minute –
For the days left.
To breathe is a boon
Till the final call comes
“Be an unmoved Zen priest
To love in leisure”
Tells thus ‘The Regime of Corona’!

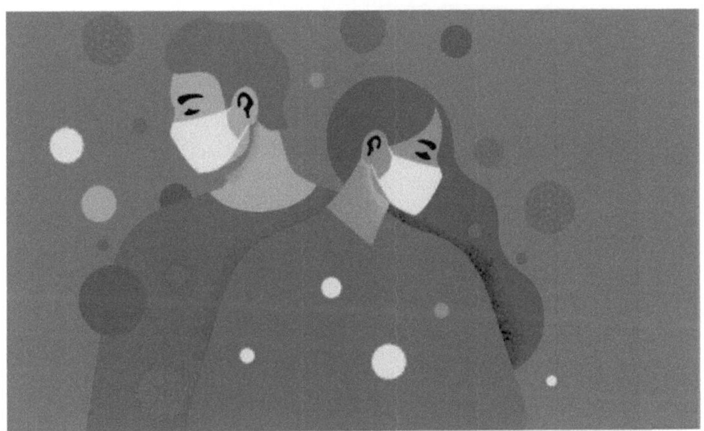

9 798889 516859

Printed by Libri Plureos GmbH in Hamburg, Germany